D1213806

THE MIRACLE OF CHRISTMAS

GOD WITH US

JOHN F. MACARTHUR, JR.

ZondervanPublishingHouse

A Division of HarperCollins*Publishers*

PROJECT EDITOR: SHERRY HARNEY

PRINTED IN HONG KONG

93 94 95 / HK / 3 2

THE MIRACLE OF CHRISTMAS

GOD WITH US

To:_____

MAY THIS BE THE MOST
WONDERFUL CHRISTMAS YOU
HAVE EVER CELEBRATED.

FROM:_____

THE HEART AND SOUL OF THE CHRISTMAS MESSAGE

IF WE COULD CONDENSE ALL THE
TRUTHS OF CHRISTMAS INTO ONLY
THREE WORDS, THESE WOULD BE
THE WORDS: "GOD WITH US."

WHAT CHRISTMAS IS REALLY
ABOUT IS THE BIRTH OF JESUS —
IMMANUEL, GOD WITH US, THE
PROMISED MESSIAH — WHO CAME
TO SAVE HIS PEOPLE FROM THEIR
SINS (MATTHEW 1:21).

WE TEND TO FOCUS OUR ATTENTION
AT CHRISTMAS ON THE INFANCY
OF CHRIST. THE GREATER TRUTH OF
THE HOLIDAY IS HIS DEITY. MORE
ASTONISHING THAN A BABY IN
THE MANGER IS THE TRUTH THAT
THIS PROMISED BABY IS THE
OMNIPOTENT CREATOR OF THE
HEAVENS AND THE EARTH.

TRUE JOY COMES FROM A
REALIZATION OF WHAT CHRISTMAS
IS REALLY ALL ABOUT AND FROM
KNOWING THE ONE WHOSE BIRTH
WE CELEBRATE.

A Christmas Prophecy

"THE LORD HIMSELF WILL GIVE
YOU A SIGN: BEHOLD, A VIRGIN WILL
BE WITH CHILD AND BEAR A SON,
AND SHE WILL CALL HIS NAME
IMMANUEL" (ISAIAH 7:14).

Isaiah foretold that Jesus would be born to a virgin and that she was to call His name Immanuel. Immanuel is a Hebrew name that means literally, "God with us." It is a promise of incarnate deity, a prophecy that God Himself would appear as a human infant, Immanuel, "God with us."

"A CHILD WILL BE BORN TO US, A SON WILL BE GIVEN TO US; AND THE GOVERNMENT WILL REST ON HIS SHOULDERS; AND HIS NAME WILL BE CALLED WONDERFUL COUNSELOR, MIGHTY GOD, ETERNAL FATHER, PRINCE OF PEACE" (ISAIAH 9:6).

"Wonderful Counselor, Mighty God, Eternal Father, Prince of Peace." Those are remarkable titles for a baby. This was no ordinary child, but one whose coming had been long awaited.

JESUS IS A WONDERFUL COUNSELOR.
HE KNOWS ALL ABOUT YOU;
HE KNOWS ALL THE NEEDS OF YOUR
HEART; HE KNOWS HOW TO ANSWER
THOSE NEEDS. AND HE ALWAYS
GIVES WISE COUNSEL TO THOSE
WHO WILL HEAR AND OBEY HIM.

JESUS IS A SOVEREIGN MASTER
WHO IS NOT DEPENDENT ON THE
WISDOM OF THIS WORLD. IT IS HE
TO WHOM WE MUST ULTIMATELY
TURN TO MAKE SENSE OF LIFE'S
CONFUSION.

JESUS IS GOD, AND BECAUSE HE IS
GOD, HE CAN FORGIVE SIN, DEFEAT
SATAN, LIBERATE PEOPLE FROM
THE POWER OF EVIL, REDEEM THEM,
ANSWER THEIR PRAYERS, RESTORE
THEIR BROKEN SOULS, AND REIGN
OVER A REBUILT LIFE, BRINGING
ORDER TO OUR CHAOS.

NOTHING IS TOO DIFFICULT FOR
THE CREATOR AND SUSTAINER OF
EVERYTHING. INFINITY AND ALL ITS
INTRICACIES ARE NOTHING TO HIM
WHO IS THE ALPHA AND OMEGA,
THE FIRST AND LAST, THE BEGINNING
AND END — THE FATHER OF ETERNITY.

THE MESSAGE OF CHRISTMAS IN
prophetic form is the good
news of God's answer to all the
confusion, chaos, complexities,
and conflicts of life. It is the
gift of One who is a newborn
infant and yet was the Father of
all eternity. He is God with us.

KNOTS ON THE
FAMILY TREE

Jesus' ancestry may surprise
you. Four women in particular
stand out. Not only is it
unusual to find women listed
in a Hebrew genealogy, but
these women are particularly
noteworthy because they
contrast so dramatically with
the absolute purity and
righteousness of God's
Anointed One.

THEIR NAMES ARE TAMAR, RAHAB,
RUTH, AND BATHSHEBA. ALL OF
THEM WERE OUTCASTS, YET THEY
MADE IT INTO JESUS' FAMILY
ALBUM. THESE WOMEN REPRESENT
TWO HARLOTS, ONE CURSED
MOABITE, AND AN ADULTERESS.
THEY ARE A STRONG ASSURANCE OF
GOD'S GRACE TO SINNERS LIKE US.

JESUS' GENEALOGY UNDERSCORES
THE TRUTH THAT JESUS IDENTIFIED
WITH SINNERS. IT PUTS A HOLY
SPOTLIGHT ON GOD'S GRACE.

WE FIND A MESSAGE OF GRACE IN
JESUS' GENEALOGY. IT IS THE HEART
OF THE CHRISTMAS STORY. GOD
IN HIS MERCY DOING FOR SINNERS
WHAT THEY CANNOT DO FOR
THEMSELVES — MENDING BROKEN
LIVES AND RESTORING SHATTERED
HOPES. THAT'S WHY HE CAME.

Is the Virgin Birth Really Essential?

No other fact in the Christmas story is more important than the virgin birth. The virgin birth must have happened exactly the way Scripture says. Otherwise, Christmas has no point at all. To deny the virgin birth is to reject Christ's deity.

IF THERE IS NO VIRGIN BIRTH,
JESUS IS NOT GOD. IF HE IS NOT
GOD, HIS CLAIMS ARE LIES. IF HIS
CLAIMS ARE LIES, HIS SALVATION IS
A HOAX. AND IF HIS SALVATION IS
A HOAX, WE ARE ALL DOOMED.

JOSEPH AND MARY

MARY'S FAITH IS A WONDERFUL
EXAMPLE FOR US. RATHER THAN
RESENTFULLY LOOKING AT HER
PREGNANCY AS UNFAIR AND
EMBARRASSING, SHE UNDERSTOOD
THAT SHE HAD BEEN UNIQUELY
BLESSED BY GOD.

JOSEPH IS A REMARKABLE EXAMPLE
OF EXTRAORDINARY FAITH.
UNDERSTANDABLY DISTRESSED
WHEN HE DISCOVERED MARY WAS
GOING TO HAVE A BABY, HE
NEVERTHELESS ACCEPTED THE
DIFFICULT CONSEQUENCES OF
GOD'S WILL FOR THEIR LIVES.

THOUGH THEY MUST HAVE
SUFFERED TREMENDOUSLY FROM
THE LIES AND INNUENDO OF CRUEL
GOSSIP-MONGERS, JOSEPH AND
MARY WERE STEADFAST. THEY
PROBABLY DIDN'T UNDERSTAND
THE FULLNESS OF GOD'S PLAN, BUT
THEY FOLLOWED UNWAVERINGLY.
THEY WERE IDEAL EARTHLY PARENTS
FOR GOD'S ONLY BEGOTTEN SON.

The People
Who Missed
Christmas

"NO ROOM." THOSE SHAMEFUL
WORDS DESCRIBE MORE THAN THE
INN IN BETHLEHEM. THEY APPLY
JUST AS APTLY TO TODAY'S WORLD.
SADLY, IN ALL THE BUSYNESS OF
OUR CHRISTMAS CELEBRATIONS,
MOST PEOPLE STILL MAKE NO
ROOM FOR JESUS.

GOD IN A MANGER

THE WORLD IS HAPPY TO LET JESUS
CHRIST BE A BABY IN A MANGER,
BUT NOT WILLING TO LET HIM BE
THE SOVEREIGN KING AND LORD
THAT HE IS. YET THAT IS THE CENTRAL
TRUTH OF THE CHRISTMAS STORY:
THE CHILD OF CHRISTMAS IS GOD.

"IN THE BEGINNING WAS THE
WORD, AND THE WORD WAS WITH
GOD, AND THE WORD WAS GOD. HE
WAS IN THE BEGINNING WITH GOD.
ALL THINGS CAME INTO BEING
THROUGH HIM; AND APART FROM
HIM NOTHING CAME INTO BEING
THAT HAS COME INTO BEING"
(JOHN 1:1-3).

THE BABE IN BETHLEHEM MADE
EVERYTHING. THIS CHILD IN THE
MANGER WAS THE INCARNATION
OF GOD.

CHRISTMAS IS A CELEBRATION OF
GOD'S LOVE TOWARD MAN. THE
BABE IN A MANGER IS MORE THAN
JUST A TENDER CHILD. HE IS THE
IMAGE OF GOD. HE TOOK ON A BODY
OF HUMAN FLESH SO THAT HE MIGHT
BEAR IN THAT BODY THE SINS OF
THE WORLD. HE MADE POSSIBLE
THE GIFT OF GOD — ETERNAL LIFE
(ROMANS 6:23).

GOD LOVES YOU, INDIVIDUALLY.
THE INCARNATION OF GOD IN JESUS
CHRIST IS NOTHING IF IT IS NOT
PERSONAL. HE CALLS YOU TO
RESPOND IN FAITH. BELIEVE HIM,
AND TRUST HIM WITH YOUR LIFE.
"HE WHO BELIEVES IN THE SON HAS
ETERNAL LIFE" (JOHN 3:36).

THE GREATEST GIFT YOU CAN
EVER RECEIVE IS "BEING JUSTIFIED
AS A GIFT BY HIS GRACE THROUGH
THE REDEMPTION WHICH IS IN
CHRIST JESUS" (ROMANS 3:24).

No sin, no matter how heinous, puts sinners beyond Jesus' reach. Jesus is saving His people from their sins. "He is able to save forever those who draw near to God through Him, since He always lives to make intercession for them" (Hebrews 7:25).

Who Were the Wise Men?

THE MAGI WERE TRUE WISE MEN.
"THEY FELL DOWN AND WORSHIPED
HIM" (MATTHEW 2:11).
WHILE JESUS' OWN PEOPLE DID NOT
COME TO SEE HIM, THIS GROUP OF
GENTILE MYSTICS RECOGNIZED AND
WORSHIPED THE KING OF THE JEWS.

Born To Die

HERE'S A SIDE TO THE CHRISTMAS
STORY THAT ISN'T OFTEN TOLD:
JESUS WAS BORN TO DIE.

On that very first Christmas, earth was oblivious to all that was happening. But heaven wasn't. The holy angels were waiting in anticipation to break forth in praise and worship and adoration at the birth of the newborn Child. This Child's birth meant deliverance for mankind.

THE IMPORTANT ISSUE OF
CHRISTMAS IS NOT SO MUCH THAT
JESUS CAME, BUT WHY HE CAME.
HE CAME TO DIE. THERE WAS A
PRICE TO BE PAID FOR OUR SINS.
SOMEONE HAD TO DIE. ONLY
JESUS COULD DO IT.

JESUS' SOFT LITTLE HANDS,
FASHIONED BY THE HOLY SPIRIT
IN MARY'S WOMB, WERE MADE SO
THAT NAILS MIGHT BE DRIVEN
THROUGH THEM.

THOSE BABY FEET, PINK AND
UNABLE TO WALK, WOULD ONE DAY
WALK UP A DUSTY HILL TO BE
NAILED TO A CROSS.

THAT SWEET INFANT'S HEAD WITH
SPARKLING EYES AND EAGER MOUTH
WAS FORMED SO THAT SOMEDAY
MEN MIGHT FORCE A CROWN OF
THORNS ONTO IT.

THAT TENDER BODY, WARM AND
SOFT, WRAPPED IN SWADDLING
CLOTHES, WOULD ONE DAY BE
RIPPED OPEN BY A SPEAR.

TAKE ANOTHER LOOK AT THE
MANGER THIS CHRISTMAS. LOOK
BEYOND THE TENDER SCENE,
AND SEE WHAT JESUS HIMSELF
KNEW EVEN BEFORE HE CAME —
THAT HE WAS BORN TO DIE.

JESUS DIED FOR YOU. HE BORE YOUR SIN. HE PURCHASED YOUR SALVATION. HE GUARANTEED YOUR SANCTIFICATION. HE DESTROYED YOUR ENEMY. AND HE BECAME A SYMPATHETIC HIGH PRIEST. HE IS READY TO MAKE INTERCESSION FOR YOU.

JESUS' DEATH, THOUGH DEVISED
AND CARRIED OUT BY MEN WITH
EVIL INTENTIONS, WAS IN NO SENSE
A TRAGEDY. IN FACT, IT REPRESENTS
THE GREATEST VICTORY OVER EVIL
ANYONE HAS EVER ACCOMPLISHED.

WHEN JESUS DIED ON THE CROSS, HE ABSORBED THE FULL PENALTY OF SIN. IF WE WERE TO SUFFER HELL FOR ALL ETERNITY, WE WOULD NEVER PAY THE FULL PRICE. BUT HE GATHERED UP AN ETERNITY OF PUNISHMENT, PAID IT ALL, AND WALKED AWAY FROM IT A RISEN SAVIOR. THAT IS POWER!

JESUS DIDN'T COME BECAUSE
WE ASKED FOR OR DESERVED HIS
INTERVENTION, BUT BECAUSE HE IS
A GOD OF GRACE. HIS LOVINGKIND-
NESS TOWARD US IS ABSOLUTELY
UNDESERVED. CHRIST CHOSE TO DIE
FOR US SOLELY ON THE BASIS OF
HIS SOVEREIGN GOOD WILL.

EVEN WHEN JESUS CAME TO EARTH
AND THE MASS OF PEOPLE REJECTED
HIM, MOCKED HIM, HATED HIM,
AND EVEN KILLED HIM, THAT DIDN'T
STIFLE HIS GRACE. AS HE DIED, HE
PRAYED, "FATHER, FORGIVE THEM;
FOR THEY DO NOT KNOW WHAT THEY
ARE DOING" (LUKE 23:34).

"HE IS NOT ASHAMED TO CALL THEM BRETHREN" (HEBREW 2:11). CHRIST CALLS US BROTHERS. WE ARE PART OF THE SAME FAMILY. THERE IS NO HIERARCHY AMONG BROTHERS. THIS VERSE IS SAYING WE ARE ONE WITH CHRIST. WE ARE AS ACCEPTABLE TO GOD AS IF WE WERE AS SINLESS AS CHRIST.

O Come Let Us
Adore Him

THE FIRST PRIORITY IN ALL
OUR CELEBRATING AT CHRISTMAS
SHOULD BE WORSHIP, AND
EVERYTHING ELSE WE DO SHOULD
FLOW OUT OF ADORING HEARTS.

CHRISTMAS SHOULD BE A TIME
OF REAL JOY AND GLADNESS, AS
OPPOSED TO THE MANUFACTURED
SENTIMENT AND WILD REVELRY
THAT CHARACTERIZES THE WAY THE
WORLD OBSERVES CHRISTMAS.

GOD HAS GIVEN THE GREATEST
CHRISTMAS GIFT OF ALL TIME:
"FOR GOD SO LOVED THE WORLD,
THAT HE GAVE HIS ONLY BEGOTTEN
SON, THAT WHOEVER BELIEVES IN
HIM SHOULD NOT PERISH, BUT HAVE
ETERNAL LIFE" (JOHN 3:16).

AND CHRIST GAVE HIS ALL FOR US:
"ALTHOUGH HE EXISTED IN THE
FORM OF GOD, HE DID NOT REGARD
EQUALITY WITH GOD A THING TO
BE GRASPED, BUT EMPTIED
HIMSELF, TAKING THE FORM OF A
BOND-SERVANT, AND BEING MADE
IN THE LIKENESS OF MEN"
(PHILIPPIANS 2:6-7).